D1117194

Discovering Mission
Santa Cruz

BY SOFIA NUÑES

Cavendish
Square

New York

Published in 2015 by Cavendish Square Publishing, LLC
243 5th Avenue, Suite 136, New York, NY 10016

Library of Congress Cataloging-in-Publication Data

Nuñes, Sofia.
Discovering Mission Santa Cruz / Sofia Nuñes.
pages cm. — (California missions)
Includes index.
ISBN 978-1-62713-070-7 (hardcover) ISBN 978-1-62713-072-1 (ebook)
1. Santa Cruz Mission—History—Juvenile literature. 2. Spanish mission buildings—California—Santa Cruz—History—Juvenile literature. 3. Franciscans—California—Santa Cruz—History—Juvenile literature. 4. Ohlone Indians—Missions—California—Santa Cruz—History—Juvenile literature. 5. California—History—To 1846—Juvenile literature. 6. Santa Cruz (Calif.)—History—Juvenile literature. I. Title.

F869.S48O88 2014
979.4'71—dc23

2014003430

Editorial Director: Dean Miller
Editor: Kristen Susienka
Copy Editor: Cynthia Roby
Art Director: Jeffrey Talbot
Designer: Douglas Brooks
Photo Researcher: J8 Media
Production Manager: Jennifer Ryder-Talbot
Production Editor: David McNamara

The photographs in this book are used by permission and through the courtesy of: Cover photo by Mariusz Jurgielewicz/Shutterstock.com; Lowe R. Llaguno/Shutterstock.com, 1; Nagel Photography/Shutterstock.com, 4; Master of Saldana/The Bridgeman Art Library/Getty Images, 6; Ann Thiermann/Dancing at Quiroste/Ann Thiermann, 8-9; Danita Delimont/Gallo Images/Getty Images, 10; © 2014 Pentacle Press, 12; Howcheng/Fray Junipero Serra statue, Mission San Buenaventura.JPG/Wikimedia Commons, 13; Courtesy of UC Berkeley, Bancroft Library, 16; Courtesy of UC Berkeley, Bancroft Library, 19; © 2012 Pentacle Press, 21; North Wind Picture Archives/Alamy, 22; North Wind Picture Archives/Alamy, 24; North Wind Picture Archives/Alamy, 26; North Wind/North Wind Picture Archives, 29; Ann Thiermann/Quiroste Mural/Ann Thiermann, 30; Courtesy of UC Berkeley, Bancroft Library, 32-33; Rachel Titiriga/File:Mission Complex Santa Cruz.jpg/Wikimedia Commons, 34; RES Photo Services, 36; Lowe R. Llaguno/Shutterstock.com, 41.

Printed in the United States of America

CALIFORNIA
MISSIONS

Contents

Mission Santa Cruz is remembered today by its church and few other mission buildings.

1
The Spanish Expand Their Empire

MISSION SANTA CRUZ

Today, the small, busy city of Santa Cruz is home to more than 60,000 people who have access to schools, libraries, shops, and parks. Santa Cruz also is home to something that might get lost in its surroundings, something that played a big part in its rich and exciting history.

On Mission Hill, just a few blocks from downtown, stands a small, one-story building. There is nothing fancy about its appearance. The walls are white. The roof is red. There is nothing that hints at the role this building played in the beginning of the city of Santa Cruz or of its place in the history of the state of California. This modest structure is the last remaining building of Mission Santa Cruz.

COLUMBUS REACHES THE AMERICAS

Christopher Columbus returned to Spain from his 1492 voyage to the New World (North America, the Caribbean, South America,

Spanish explorers such as Hernán Cortés landed in the New World and claimed land for Spain.

and Central America), with gold, parrots, spices, and human captives. This made the Spanish eager to explore the land. They were hoping to find gold, great cities, and a faster trade route to Asia, where they could buy silks and spices to sell for high prices in Europe.

In 1519, a Spanish soldier and explorer named Hernán Cortés brought ships, guns, horses, and soldiers to the land that is now known as Mexico. There, in 1521, he conquered the great Aztec empire for Spain. Spain named this land **New Spain** and set up a government under an official called a **viceroy**, who acted in place of the king.

In 1542, Viceroy Mendoza of New Spain sent explorer Juan Rodríguez Cabrillo by boat up the California coast in search of a river that cut through North America and to claim land for Spain. Cabrillo found a harbor that today is San Diego Bay. Cabrillo died on the expedition after a fall on San Miguel Island, but his crew continued heading north and made the first maps of the California coast. His crew didn't find the river or any riches, so the viceroy decided not to send more ships there. The Spanish would not return to what they called **Alta California** for 160 years. *Alta* in Spanish means "upper." "Lower," or *Baja* California, is a long peninsula that is now part of Mexico.

2
The
Ohlone

LAND OF PLENTY

When the Spanish arrived in what they named Santa Cruz, the area was filled with hills, prairies, swampland, beaches, and tall oak and redwood forests. Many tribes of **indigenous people**—people native-born to a particular region or environment—lived through-out the area, and few spoke the same language. The Spanish called them *Costanoans*, or "coastal people." Today, these tribes choose to be known collectively as the Ohlone.

Like most of the indigenous people of California, the Ohlone lived by hunting, fishing, and gathering. The forests were filled with acorns, a staple of the Ohlone diet. Acorns were ground between two stones and turned into flour, which was boiled to make a thick cereal or used to make bread.

The Ohlone women gathered fruits and vegetables. The men hunted birds and game animals. They also found food in the Pacific Ocean and in the nearby rivers.

The Ohlone were nomads, moving to find a food source that was in season. Since they moved around so often, they built homes that were meant to last for only a short time. To build them, the

The Ohlone lived in villages and built their homes from trees and reeds around them.

Ohlone placed long willow branches into the ground and tied the tops to a dome. Then, they weaved branches through the sides to create walls. A small hole was left in the roof to allow smoke from a small cooking fire to escape.

The men and boys of the Ohlone tribes wore little or no clothing in the warmer months. Women and girls wore decorated skirts. All wore deerskin, rabbitskin, or seal-skin cloaks when it turned cold. Ohlone men and women wore earrings and nose rings made of shells, and necklaces made of shells and feathers. They wore their hair piled on their heads, and painted lines and dots on their faces.

NATIVE JOBS

Trading was important to the Ohlone tribes. It allowed them to get things they could not find in their area. For example, a tribe from the forests in the interior might trade pine nuts for shells or

salt from tribes close to the ocean. Among the other items traded were beads made from shells, arrowheads, strong wood for making weapons, and dyes for creating paints. The trader was such an important figure that when he arrived at different villages to trade, he was often welcomed with ceremonies and songs.

Another task important to the Ohlone was basket weaving. Baskets were used for cooking, carrying water, and gathering food. Ohlone women used sticks and grass to make their baskets, and often decorated them with shells and beads. The Ohlone considered basket weaving to be an art form.

BELIEFS AND PRACTICES

There is very little known about the religious practices of the Ohlone because they did not write them down. Instead, these traditions were passed down from generation to generation verbally.

The Ohlone made unique baskets to help them carry items and water over long distances.

Historians do know that every tribe had a *shaman*—a powerful healer and spiritual leader in Native American culture. A shaman was believed to cure illness through medicine, dance, and prayer.

The Ohlone believed that spirits lived in everything around them, including animals, trees, and the earth. Their goal was to maintain peace with these spirits. The Ohlone tribes were organized by villages, which could be home to as many as 50 to 500 inhabitants. Families were combined into groups called clans. Each of these clans had their own animal spirits, and clan members never hunted or ate those animals.

Dance and music were important parts of Ohlone religion and culture. The Ohlone played handmade whistles, flutes, and rattles. They celebrated births, deaths, weddings, hunts, and religious days with music and dancing. The Ohlone believed that if they respected and celebrated what they took from nature, nature would be kind in return.

3
The
Mission System

FORCED TO ACT

The Spanish returned to Alta California when the Russians and British began to settle there. They wanted to make sure the region would always belong to Spain. On January 7, 1769, the first of three ships carrying supplies set out for the harbor that Cabrillo had found in Alta California. Four months later, on May 15, a group of men set out on horseback to meet the ships. Their 715-mile (1150-kilometer) journey began at Mission Santa Maria in Baja California, and passed through several desert areas.

The Spanish had learned from their wars against the Aztecs and the Mayans that it was better to try to get along with the Native people than to fight with them. They wanted to **convert** the Native Americans to **Christianity** and teach them aspects of Spanish culture, which they considered superior. They also formed a different plan for **colonizing** Alta California than the strategies used in other regions. Instead of bringing in settlers to colonize the area, they hoped the Native Americans would learn how to farm the land and become citizens of Spain. (This never happened, however.)

To attempt this, the Spanish set up missions. The Spanish were Catholic, and when they colonized Alta California they brought **missionaries** from the **Franciscan** order called **friars**, or *frays* in Spanish. Although the Spanish leaders wanted to build missions to claim more land for Spain, the friars went to the missions because they wanted to help people. Catholics believed that anyone who did not believe in Christianity would not go to heaven. The friars became missionaries because they wanted to teach people to believe in Christianity so that they could go to heaven.

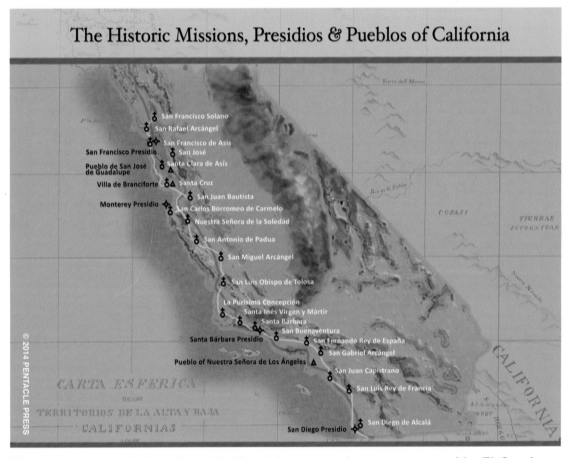

The twenty-one missions lined California's coast and were connected by El Camino Real (indicated by the yellow line on the map). Four presidios were also started.

Fray Junípero Serra was the first leader of the Alta California mission system.

FOUNDING FATHER

Among the men who took the overland trip to meet the supply ships was a fifty-five-year-old friar named Junípero Serra. Fray Serra had taught philosophy on the island of Majorca near Spain before the Franciscans sent him to New Spain in 1751. He was a devoted priest, and success-fully converted many Native Americans to Christianity. In recognition of this success, Fray Serra was chosen to be the first president of the Alta California missions to be built along the Pacific Coast.

Fray Serra founded nine Alta California missions before his death in 1784. After Fray Serra died, Fray Fermín Francisco de Lasuén became president of the Alta California missions. It was Fray Lasuén who would found Mission Santa Cruz.

In all, twenty-one missions were built between July 1769 and July 1823.

4
Mission Santa Cruz Begins

HOLY CROSS

In the 1700s, the area around the San Lorenzo River was beautiful and lush. Sycamore, cottonwood, and willow trees lined the river's banks, and there was lots of grass and forests nearby. The land was fertile, and many Ohlone villages were located close to the area.

In 1790, the viceroy of New Spain asked Fray Lasuén to found a mission in this area. The viceroy gave Fray Lasuén 1,000 pesos to buy supplies, and provided an additional 400 pesos to pay the travel expenses of the two friars who would live at the mission.

On August 28, 1791, Fray Lasuén sprinkled holy water on the chosen site and named the twelfth mission Santa Cruz, which means, "Holy Cross." As with all the missions, a cross made of wood was set in the ground and a **Mass** was held. With Fray Lasuén were six soldiers from the San Francisco *presidio*. Presidios were military forts for soldiers built along the Pacific Coast.

A number of Ohlone people from nearby villages attended the founding ceremony. Fray Lasuén wrote the viceroy to say that he was pleased at how many Ohlone had come, and that he thought that many of them would gladly join the mission. Mission Santa Cruz was officially founded—however it was a few weeks before there was anything on the site but the wooden cross.

On September 24, 1791, Native Americans from Mission Santa Clara de Asís came to Mission Santa Cruz to help put up temporary huts. The two friars who would live at the mission, Fray Isidro Alonzo Salazar and Fray Baldomero López, then held another founding ceremony. This ceremony was more formal, and more people were there to see it. A chief from a nearby village, Chief Sugert, brought his daughters and a few members of his tribe to the ceremony. They would be the first Ohlone people converted to Christianity. The Spanish called the newly converted Native Americans **neophytes**. Neophyte is a Greek word that means "new converted."

There are several theories on why the Native Americans joined missions such as Mission Santa Cruz and became neophytes. Some followed their chiefs when they converted to Christianity. Others may have been attracted by the material goods of the Spanish, such as cloth and objects made out of metal. And some Native Americans may have been drawn by the knowledge and skills of the Spanish and the hope of creating a powerful ally, which would be useful in wars with other tribes. These skills, such as their mastery over the horse, implied that the visitors had some supernatural power.

After the two friars held Mass, the leader of the San Francisco presidio gave a speech, claiming the land for Spain. Then, the soldiers fired their guns into the air, and the founding ceremony was complete. The friars invited the Ohlone to help build the temporary shelters, promising they would be paid with blankets and maize. The shelters went up quickly.

A GOOD START

Operations at Mission Santa Cruz started smoothly. Animals, grains, and supplies were brought from nearby missions so that farming could begin. The friars conducted their first **baptism**,

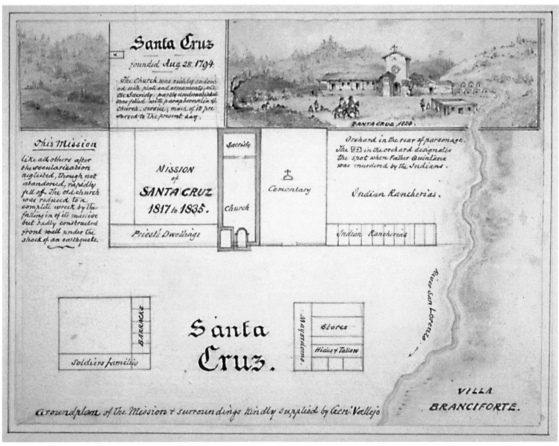

This ground plan of the mission, drawn in the 1830s, illustrates what the mission looked like back then.

which initiates a person into Christianity, on October 9, 1791.

A few months later, the San Lorenzo River flooded and the buildings at Mission Santa Cruz were damaged. Instead of repairing the buildings, the friars decided to rebuild on higher ground. They were afraid the mission might flood again. New temporary shelters had to be built.

Although the mission had some problems, there were still a number of the indigenous people who wanted to join. By December 1791, the friars had baptized nineteen adults and sixty-eight children. The Ohlone had built temporary housing for the friars and a temporary church. Farming had also been successful, and they had fenced in the livestock and planted an orchard.

Once the basics of mission life were established, the Ohlone began building the permanent church. Soldiers taught the Ohlone how to make **adobe** bricks from water, mud, and straw. This mixture was packed into rectangular molds and set in the sun to dry. Once dry, the bricks could be removed from the molds and stored.

The permanent church's cornerstone was laid on February 27, 1793. A year later, building was almost finished. The Ohlone people building it worked hard constructing the foundation out of stone and forming the walls out of adobe bricks they had made. When the church was finished it was 29 feet (7.6 m) wide, 112 feet (34.1 m) long, and 25 feet (8.8 m) high. On May 10, 1794, Mission Santa Cruz was dedicated, and the first Mass there was held the following day.

5
Early Days at Mission Santa Cruz

TROUBLES ARISE

A great start at Mission Santa Cruz gave no warning of the troubles to come. There were many early Native American conversions to Christianity. Within the first three months, there were eighty-seven neophytes at the mission. By 1796, there were 523. Within six years of the founding of the mission, its quadrangle was completed, and featured workshops and a granary.

The mission was very productive, but all was not well. Since its founding, a number of the friars who came to live and do missionary work became unhappy and left after just a year or so. It seems that the Ohlone were not happy with the mission either. In 1796, one of the friars wrote to the presidio at San Francisco to ask for more soldiers to come and protect the mission from the threat of Native American attacks. Such attacks were usually rare, as the indigenous people in Alta California were mostly peaceful.

UNWELCOME GUESTS

Problems grew after the governor of Alta California decided to build a pueblo, or settlement, just across the river from Mission

Spanish explorers traveled throughout the new California territory.

Santa Cruz in an effort to bring more Spanish settlers to the area. The pueblo was the first of three built in Alta California by Spain. The others were in San Jose and Los Angeles. A fourth pueblo was built in Sonoma by Mexico in the 1830s.

The pueblos were designed to be farming communities and to supply the presidios with food. Much of the food grown in the area was being sent to what is now Mexico.

On May 12, 1797, seventeen settlers from New Spain arrived, and the town called Villa de Branciforte was established. These first settlers were criminals. Some were given a choice between settling in Villa de Branciforte or going to jail. Over the next year, more Spanish settlers arrived at the town, drawn by a promotion that promised them a house. These houses were never built. By September 1799, forty men lived in Villa de Branciforte.

The governor had hoped to attract craftsmen who would start businesses and bring families to the town. Instead, the men at Villa de Branciforte did no work. They drank, played cards, and fought. They built a racetrack. The settlers used money to try to lure the Ohlone away from the mission so that they could use them to work on their buildings or in their fields. They also took over some Ohlone pastureland, angering the indigenous people.

The friars were upset that Villa de Branciforte had been built so close to their mission. Settlements weren't supposed to be built within seven miles of a mission, and this one was just across the river. They felt that the unruly settlers were a bad influence on the neophytes of Mission Santa Cruz.

Villa de Branciforte suffered from many problems and eventually disappeared. The other seven pueblos and presidios survived to be recognized by the United States.

THE NEOPHYTES ESCAPE

Mission Santa Cruz was the smallest of the California missions, with 523 neophytes living there during its peak. However, in 1797, heavy rains destroyed part of the church and damaged other buildings. Much work needed to be done to complete the repairs. By this time, many neophytes were tired of working at the mission. They missed the freedom of their old life in their villages. That year, 138 neophytes escaped from the mission. Some managed to hide from the soldiers who were sent to find them, but ninety Ohlone people were hunted down and brought back to the mission. These neophytes were punished and forced to return to work.

In 1798, more neophytes escaped, leaving only about thirty-five at the mission. The friars were distraught. The mission's lands were overflowing with water. The livestock were dying. To top it all off, a dead whale washed up on the beach that year. The whale's carcass attracted an unusually large number of wolves and bears, which posed a threat to the farm animals in the area. Mission Santa Cruz, whose beginnings had held such promise, would never truly recover from the setbacks suffered during this time.

Natives that left the mission faced many hardships and found they could not return to their old way of life.

6
Daily Life at Mission Santa Cruz

LIVING WITHIN RULES

The Ohlone way of life changed when a person joined the mission. Once baptized, the neophytes could practice no other religion but Catholicism, not even the faith they had known their whole lives.

A strict schedule of daily prayer and hard work was kept by all who lived at the missions.

Religious life, as practiced by the Franciscans and other Catholic orders, was dictated by a set of rules. The friars imposed rules on the neophytes and forced them to follow a strict schedule. It is unclear if many of the Native Americans understood these conditions before they agreed to be baptized.

The neophytes were never allowed to leave

the mission without permission. According to Spanish customs, women were locked in their quarters at night, and neophytes who did not do their work were beaten, put in leg irons, or jailed.

Unmarried women and girls over the age of eleven lived together in the mission building, in an area called a *monjerío*. Much of the women's work was done in the monjerío. Families and unmarried men lived in housing just outside the mission, called *rancherías*.

A Life of Structure

An average day at Mission Santa Cruz followed this schedule:

6:00 A.M.	The mission bells rang to wake everyone at the mission and at the rancherías.
6:01 A.M.	Time for prayers.
6:30 A.M.	Breakfast.
7:00 A.M.	The bells rang to call everyone to work.
12:00 P.M.	Lunch.
1:00 P.M.	A rest period, called a *siesta*.
3:00 P.M.	Everyone returned to work.
5:00 P.M.	Dinner.
6:00 P.M.	Evening prayers.
7:00 P.M.	Free time.
8:00 P.M.	Bedtime for women.
9:00 P.M.	Bedtime for men.

CHANGE IN LIFESTYLE

When they joined the mission, the Native Americans had to give up an entire way of life. Food was so plentiful in the region that the Ohlone just had to gather it to eat. At the mission, the Ohlone men were taught to farm and grow their food. This changed their diet.

As nomads, the Ohlone had moved from place to place, living in temporary shelters. At the mission, however, they lived in one place in more permanent houses. The men were taught how to be

Many things changed for the Native people at the mission: they were educated in Spanish ways, given new food to eat, and new clothes to wear.

builders, blacksmiths, and how to make leather goods and tools. Their people had survived for centuries without these skills.

The friars also forced the indigenous people to change the way they dressed. The lack of clothing worn by the Native Americans made the friars uncomfortable, so they were ordered to dress the way the Spaniards did.

The women were taught to weave cloth, spin thread, and to sew so they could make this new style of clothing. They also prepared food and made soap and candles.

Large stones for a mill were ordered from the nearby Mission San Carlos Borroméo, and a millhouse was constructed. By the fall of 1798, the mill was in operation. Having a mill was important—now the people at the mission could grind their own corn and flour. This was a big improvement over the method used by the Natives, who used a traditional mortar and pestle. However, they no longer ground acorns.

By 1794, a granary had been built to store grain, and rooms were built for weaving. Crops were plentiful, thanks to the rich soil. That year, the Mission Santa Cruz missionaries recorded that 600 bushels of corn, sixty bushels of beans, and 1,200 bushels of grain were grown at the mission. Their crops were so plentiful that they even had extra to send to other missions, including Mission San Carlos Borroméo.

The men no longer hunted for meat or went fishing. Instead, they tended livestock, which were healthy and had plenty to eat. Mission Santa Cruz had one of the smallest livestock herds and farm output among the missions. The largest of the missions,

San Luis Rey de Francia, had a herd of 57,380 cattle and sheep, and had grown 411,000 bushels of grain and produce by 1832. By comparison, Mission Santa Cruz had a herd of only 9,236 in 1832, and had grown only 75,000 bushels of grain and produce.

The friars taught religious studies to the children. They also taught music to the brightest neophytes, showing them how to play instruments such as the violin, flute, horn, and harp. The friars oversaw all of the work done by the neophytes at the mission—and did everything they could to ensure that they would not run away from Mission Santa Cruz.

At the mission, women often weaved baskets, while men tended to livestock or built structures. Children helped where they could.

7
Beginning of the End

FIRST AUTOPSY IN CALIFORNIA

The mission, damaged in 1797, was in disrepair for years. One reason for this was there were so few neophytes to do the work.

Many were driven away by cruelty and poor conditions. One visitor to Mission San Carlos Borroméo, Jean-François de la Pérouse, wrote in his journal in 1786 that conditions there reminded him of those he'd seen in the slave colonies of the Caribbean. He described men and women in irons or placed in stocks, and wrote that he witnessed them being whipped.

Some of the friars at Santa Cruz were known for their harsh punishment. They were said to whip neophytes for small actions, including forgetting prayers or working too slowly. They were hard on captured runaways. In addition to the large group of runaways in 1798, there were fifty runaways in 1809 and 104 in 1819. The last group of runaways was from the Yokut tribe, who had been brought to the mission against their will by the friars.

The friars asked for soldiers to help rebuild the damaged mission. By 1810, a large monjerío with two wings was built for women and girls.

On October 12, 1812, one of the friars at the mission, Fray Quintana, was found dead in his bed. He had been sick for some time, so it was at first believed that he died of natural causes.

Two years later, rumors that Fray Quintana had been murdered started to spread. The friar had not been well liked. He was known to be cruel, and had beaten neophytes with whips tipped with wire. His cruelty had led some neophytes to stop speaking Spanish and to stop working.

A new investigation of the case began. The first autopsy in California history was performed on Fray Quintana's body, and it was determined that he had been strangled or suffocated. It was thought that the friar had been called out of bed to help a sick man in the orchard. He was then surrounded by some neophytes who killed him. Nine neophytes were caught and blamed for the murder. Five were sentenced to 200 lashes with a whip, and to work in chains for as long as ten years. The others died in prison. The case and resulting punishment of the neophytes further damaged the relationship between the friars and the Ohlone people.

BETRAYED BY THEIR OWN

In 1818, French pirate Hippolyte de Bouchard raided the presidio at Monterey. He and his crew stole many valuables and burned buildings there. It was feared that he was moving toward Mission Santa Cruz. On November 21, 1818, Governor de Sola of Alta California ordered the friars at Mission Santa Cruz to move everyone out of the mission. Fray Ramón Olbés and all the neophytes went to Mission Santa Clara de Asís for safety.

Despite all the hardships, neophytes were still expected to attend mass.

Governor de Sola asked the Villa de Branciforte authorities to pack up the valuables at the mission while the friars and the neophytes escaped. The governor wanted to make sure that the expensive possessions would not fall into the hands of the pirates.

Instead of safeguarding the valuables, the people of Villa de Branciforte stole them. Then they looted and set fire to some of the mission buildings, even destroying sacred objects in the church. The pirate Bouchard never arrived at Mission Santa Cruz.

ILLNESSES

Fray Olbés, who had arrived in 1818, was very discouraged by the events unfolding at Mission Santa Cruz. After the looting, he threatened to abandon the mission forever. When some of the Villa de Branciforte looters were caught and punished, however, he agreed to stay.

Mission Santa Cruz, however, continued to have severe problems. Fray Olbés was very cruel, and was not trusted by the neophytes. It is believed that he even ordered severe punishment

Each mission's population was affected by illnesses such as smallpox and measles, and many people died.

for children. Also, European diseases were killing the neophytes. The California indigenous people had never before been exposed to illnesses such as measles, mumps, or scarlet fever, and their bodies could not fight them. The friars tried to find cures, but were unsuccessful. Even the shamans couldn't help their people. The Ohlone population at the Santa Cruz mission was hurt even more by an epidemic of smallpox. Many neophytes who did not get sick were scared of the deadly diseases and ran away from the mission. Disease could be blamed for up to sixty percent of the loss of the neophyte population at all the Alta California missions combined.

To replace the lost Ohlone neophytes, the Santa Cruz missionaries searched for other Native American tribes to recruit new members. They came upon the Yokut, who were not interested in joining. The missionaries forced them to join, which was against the law, and took the Yokut to Mission Santa Cruz against their will. One hundred and four of the Yokut neophytes would run away from the mission in 1819.

8
Secularization

NEW RULERS, NEW RULES

New Spain gained its independence from Spain in 1821. It was renamed Mexico.

By this time, the missions controlled about one-third of the land in Alta California, and housed about 30,000 inhabitants. However, so many settlers were moving into the region that the mission system was no longer necessary. These new settlers also wanted control of the mission lands.

The Mexican government decided to **secularize** the missions, and in 1833 passed a law to do so. This meant that the valuable land and the livestock would be taken from the Catholic Church. Also, the churches would now be run not by missionaries, but by parish priests. These priests would not be able to make rules for California indigenous people such as the Ohlone.

Mission Santa Cruz was one of the first missions to be secularized. The Ohlone neophytes were told that they could leave Mission Santa Cruz, and they were given some livestock and land. They were soon cheated out of this land, however, and it was granted to farmers and settlers instead.

The Franciscans came to Alta California with the best of intentions, yet they failed to meet their goals for several reasons.

For example, the Native Americans needed more than ten years to adapt to the Spanish ways. The most important reason, however, was the fact that European diseases killed so many of the Native Americans. Before the Spanish arrived in Alta California, there were an estimated 300,000 Native Americans there. By 1834, records show that number had dropped to 20,000. Unlike in other regions, the indigenous people of California were not killed in large numbers in war.

By the time of secularization, the Ohlone had lived at the mission for too long to return to their former way of life. Their villages and culture were gone, and so was the social organization that had

After secularization, Mission Santa Cruz was neglected and many buildings fell into ruin.

helped them survive for centuries. Many ex-neophytes still needed the friars for guidance, but the friars were sent away by the Mexican government.

A smallpox epidemic reduced the Native American population around Mission Santa Cruz from around 300 in 1832 to 71 in 1839. The remaining Ohlone tried to live off a small portion of land that was left, but were eventually forced out by new settlers.

Lorenzo Asisara, an Ohlone man born at Mission Santa Cruz in 1820, said in an interview years later that the Mexican officials took everything, and that few ex-neophytes were given any land.

9
The Mission Alive Today

THE UNITED STATES TAKES OVER CALIFORNIA

The United States fought a war with Mexico over the territory of Alta California. The United States won the war in 1848, and in 1850 California became the thirty-first state. In 1859, President James Buchanan gave Mission Santa Cruz back to the Catholic Church. In 1863, President Abraham Lincoln signed an act that stated that all twenty-one California missions were once again the property of the Catholic Church.

Without the friars, the mission buildings suffered from neglect, and were further harmed by settlers who stole roofing tiles and wood beams to build their own homes. Without roofs for protection, some adobe missions were dissolved by rain.

An earthquake caused the bell tower at Mission Santa Cruz to fall in 1840. The tower housed nine or ten bells valued in 1835 at $3,500, the highest value for any of the missions. All of them have been lost. Another earthquake in 1857 caused the entire church to collapse.

Holy Cross Church is part of a lasting legacy of the California mission system.

A frame church was built in 1858 at Mission Santa Cruz, and was eventually replaced in 1889 by a brick structure that is in use today. It is called Holy Cross Parish.

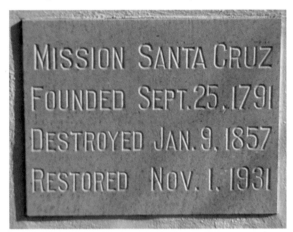

A plaque commemorates the history of Mission Santa Cruz.

A smaller version of Mission Santa Cruz's church, one-third the original size, was built near the original site in 1931. It was modeled after drawings and paintings of the original mission. Although most of the artifacts from the original mission were destroyed in earthquakes, some still remain. There is a wing attached to the church that holds them, including a 1797 painting of Our Lady of Guadalupe and some vestments (clothing and accessories worn by priests during Mass).

The mission church is a popular choice for Catholic weddings.

A small adobe building nearby, built by the Yokut people in 1824 as housing for the neophytes, is the only remaining mission housing left standing in California. This building became the headquarters of the Santa Cruz Mission State Historic Park. A museum was opened inside in 1991, 200 years after the mission was built, to teach people about mission life.

Today, the museum welcomes visitors and offers many activities—talking to volunteers, helping make candles, and learning about California's history. On certain days, you'll find volunteers dressed as people from the mission era. Overall, this is a great place to visit.

10
Make Your Own Mission Model

To make your own model of Mission Santa Cruz, you will need:

- beeswax sheets (from a craft store)
- cardboard
- corrugated cardboard
- glue
- masking tape
- miniature gold bell
- ruler
- toothpicks
- white paint
- wire mesh
- woodcraft sticks
- X-ACTO® knife (ask for an adult's help)

DIRECTIONS

Adult supervision is suggested.

Step 1: Use a piece of cardboard at least 20" × 15" (50.8 cm × 38.1 cm) for your base.

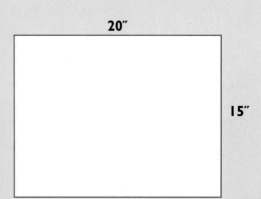

20″

15″

Step 2: For the bell tower, cut out four pieces of cardboard to measure 8" × 2" (20.3 cm × 5.1 cm) each. Glue each piece to the base, so the edges form a cube. Hold each piece in place until the glue dries.

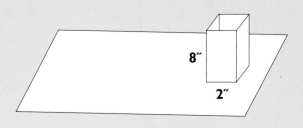

Step 3: Cut a piece of cardboard to measure 2" × 2" (5.1 cm × 5.1 cm), and glue it on top of the tower. Then, cut four pieces of cardboard to measure 2" × 1.5" (5.1 cm × 3.8 cm) each. Cut an arch shape in each piece.

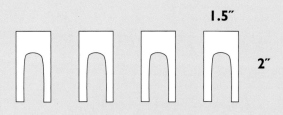

Step 4: Glue these pieces, one at a time, to the top of your tower in the shape of a square. Let dry. Place bell on a toothpick, and glue toothpick between two arches.

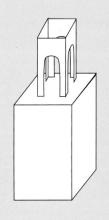

Step 5: Cut two pieces of cardboard to measure 6.6" × 8.6" (16.8 cm × 21.8 cm) each. These will be the front and back of the church.

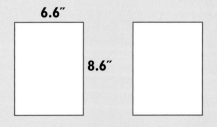

Step 6: Measure 3" (7.6 cm) down from the top and mark with a pencil on both sides. Cut diagonally from this mark to the midpoint at the top, forming a triangular shape.

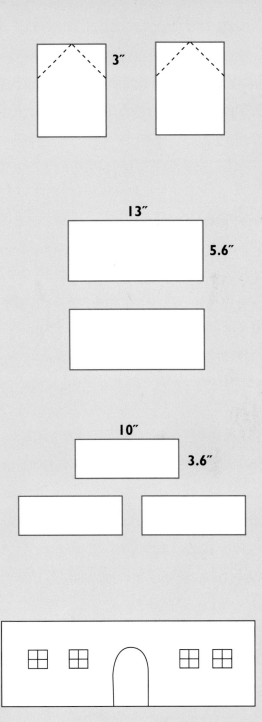

Step 7: Cut two pieces of cardboard to measure 5.6" × 13" (14.2 cm × 33 cm) each for the sides of the church. Glue all four sides in a square shape next to the tower. Hold each piece until the glue dries.

Step 8: To make the friars' quarters, cut three pieces of cardboard to measure 3.6" × 10" (9.1 cm × 25.4 cm) each for the front, back, and top.

Step 9: In one of these pieces, cut out a door and three or four windows with an X-ACTO® knife. Glue two toothpicks inside the windows in a "t" shape.

Step 10: Cut another piece of cardboard to measure 3.6" × 3.6" (9.1 cm × 9.1 cm). This is the left wall of the building (the church will make up the right side). Tape the sides together.

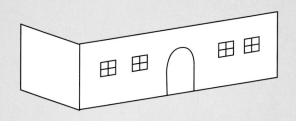

Step 11: Cut a piece of beeswax to measure 9" × 14" (22.9 cm × 35.6 cm). Bend in half the long way, and glue to the top of the church. This is the roof.

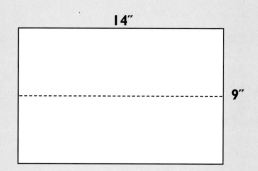

Step 12: Cut wire mesh in a circle that is 4" (10.2 cm) in diameter. Shape into half a ball and cover with a small piece of beeswax. Place on top of the tower. Make a cross out of two toothpicks and stick it in the beeswax.

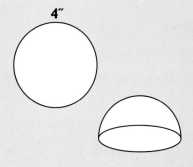

Step 13: Cut three woodcraft sticks in half lengthwise. Glue three together end to end. Repeat for the other three. These will be the top and bottom of the porch.

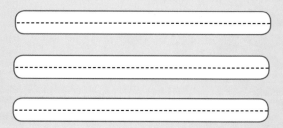

Step 14: Cut two woodcraft sticks in half and then lengthwise. Glue these between the two longer strips of sticks. Tape them in front of the friars' quarters.

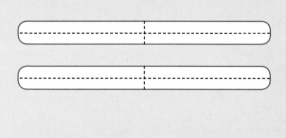

Step 15: Cut a piece of corrugated cardboard for the church door. Cut a piece of beeswax 6" × 14.6" (15.2 cm × 37.1 cm) for the roof of the friars' quarters and glue in place. Decorate as you wish with miniature flowers and trees.

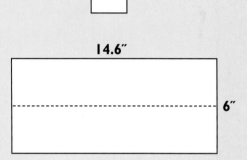

14.6"

6"

The model of Mission Santa Cruz, when completed

Key Dates in Mission History

1492	Christopher Columbus reaches the West Indies
1542	Cabrillo's expedition to California
1602	Sebastián Vizcaíno sails to California
1713	Fray Junípero Serra is born
1769	Founding of San Diego de Alcalá
1770	Founding of San Carlos Borroméo del Río Carmelo
1771	Founding of San Antonio de Padua and San Gabriel Arcángel
1772	Founding of San Luis Obispo de Tolosa
1775–76	Founding of San Juan Capistrano
1776	Founding of San Francisco de Asís
1776	Declaration of Independence is signed

1777	Founding of Santa Clara de Asís
1782	Founding of San Buenaventura
1784	Fray Serra dies
1786	Founding of Santa Bárbara
1787	Founding of La Purísima Concepción
1791	Founding of Santa Cruz and Nuestra Señora de la Soledad
1797	Founding of San José, San Juan Bautista, San Miguel Arcángel, and San Fernando Rey de España
1798	Founding of San Luis Rey de Francia
1804	Founding of Santa Inés
1817	Founding of San Rafael Arcángel
1823	Founding of San Francisco Solano
1833	Mexico passes Secularization Act
1848	Gold found in northern California
1850	California becomes the thirty-first state

Glossary

adobe (uh-DOH-bee)
Sun-dried bricks made of straw, mud, and sometimes manure.

Alta California (AL-tuh kah-lih-FOR-nyuh)
The mission area today known as the state of California.

baptism (BAP-tih-zum)
A sacrament marked by ritual use of water that makes someone a member of a Christian community and cleanses the person of his or her sins.

Christianity (kris-chee-A-nih-tee) Following the teachings of Jesus Christ and the Bible.

colonizing (KAH-luh-nyz-ing)
When people from one part of the world settle another region.

convert (kun-VERT) To change religious beliefs.

Franciscan (fran-SIS-kin)
A member of a Catholic religious group started by Saint Francis of Assisi in 1209.

friar (FRY-ur) A brother in a communal religious order. Friars can also be priests.

indigenous people (in-DIJ-en-us PEA-pel) People native-born to a particular region or environment.

Mass (MAS) The central act of worship in the Catholic Church.

missionaries (MIH-shuh-nayr-ees) Men and women who teach their religion to people with different beliefs.

neophyte (NEE-oh-fyt)
A person who has converted to another religion; Greek for "new converted."

New Spain (NOO SPAYN)
The area where the Spanish colonists had their capital in North America and that would later become Mexico.

presidio (prih-SEE-dee-oh)
A military fort built near a mission site.

secularization (seh-kyuh-luh-rih-ZAY-shun) A process by which the mission lands were made to be nonreligious.

shaman (SHAH-min)
A powerful healer and spiritual leader in Native American culture who was believed to cure illness through medicine, dance, and prayer.

viceroy (VYS-roy) A government official who rules an area as a representative of the king.

Pronunciation Guide

fray (FRAY)

monjerío (mohn-hay-REE-oh)

Ohlone (oh-LOH-nee)

pueblo (PWAY-bloh)

rancherías (rahn-cheh-REE-ahs)

siesta (see-EHS-tah)

temescal (teh-mes-KAL)

Find Out More

To learn more about the California missions, check out these books, videos, and websites:

BOOKS

Abbink, Emily. *Monterey Bay Area Missions*. Minneapolis, MN: Lerner Publishing, 2008.

Kalman, Bobbie. *Life of the California Coast Nations*. New York, NY: Crabtree Publications, 2004.

Levick, Melba, Stanley Young and Sally B. Woodbridge. *The Missions of California*. San Francisco, CA: Chronicle Books, 2004.

Weber, Francis J. *Blessed Fray Junípero Serra: An Outstanding California Hero*. Bowling Green, MO: Editions Du Signe, 2008.

VIDEOS

California Missions
www.teachertube.com/viewVideo.php?video_id=19731

Junípero Serra and the California Missions Part One
www.youtube.com/watch?v=svj7yO_EOIM

Junípero Serra and the California Missions Part Two
www.youtube.com/watch?v=6VMx27z8nfY

This two-part series features pictures of Fray Serra, detailed maps, and scenery from many of the missions he founded. This should be available in your local library. You can order by calling 1-800-876-CHIP.

WEBSITES

California Missions Foundation
www.californiamissionsfoundation.org
This website offers quick and easy facts for each mission and outlines the group that keeps the missions a part of California's history.

California Missions Resource Center
www.missionscalifornia.com
This is a website that gives great resources on all the California missions.

The Journal of San Diego History
www.sandiegohistory.org/journal/69fall/struggle.htm
This is an online website with articles about many aspects of the California mission system and people who were involved.

Cabrillo College Article – An Introduction to California's Native People
www.cabrillo.edu/~crsmith/anth6_mexicanperiod.html
This article discusses how California's Native people lived and interacted with the Spanish.

Index

Page numbers in **boldface** are illustrations.